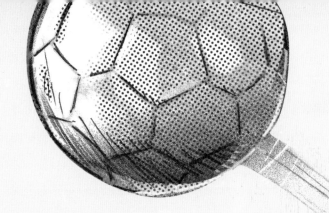

NEYMAR:

A SOCCER DREAM COME TRUE

BY **MINA JAVAHERBIN**

PICTURES BY **PAUL HOPPE**

FARRAR STRAUS GIROUX
NEW YORK

Neymarzinho runs.

Neymarzinho dribbles.

He is passing the ball to his teammate.

He is ready now.

The ball is coming toward him. It's too high for a kick, but too low for a header. He calculates, backs up, and shoots at the perfect time. The crowd goes wild.

WAAAAAA!!!

Here come the opponents!
They're getting closer to the goal.
Now they're dangerously close—
one of them shoots.

The ball is flying directly toward the goal. Wait! Who's that?
Is it Neymarzinho? Yes. He is jumping—no!—he's flying to the ball.

PHOOMp!

Neymarzinho intercepts a sure goal with an expert header. He has saved the day for Seleção, Brazil's national team.

HURRAAAAH! BRAZIL-ZIL-ZIL! *The crowd is going mad with happiness.*

"Dinnertime, everyone!" We hear my father yell, so my team and I leave the club.

I kick the ball through the narrow corridor of my grandpa's house, where we live, and all the way to the kitchen. My mother has cooked her delicious *feijoada* for Neymarzinho, the star.

"Juninho," my mother calls out to me, "can you please walk without your toy?"

"It's not a toy, Mamãe, this is a ball. I need it to train for stardom."

"Hey, Neymarzinho, it's my rice too!" my sister, Rafaela, says as I reach for the food. She is right, and I happily serve her some rice first.

After dinner, my teammates are tired—but not me, the great Neymarzinho. I go back to the club and practice by myself. First I kick with one leg and then with the other. My left leg has to be just as strong as my right.

Neymarzinho is my soccer nickname. My real name is Neymar Junior—my dad is Neymar Senior—but everyone in my family calls me Juninho, which means "junior" in Portuguese.

"Juninho," my father says to me, "one day you will be a star."

My dad's own dream of stardom ended when I was just a baby and he was injured in a car accident. But he still plays for local clubs, and we go to all his games.

I love playing soccer with him. I'm learning his expert moves.

At one of my father's matches, his friend Betinho, an indoor soccer coach, sees me sprint up and down the bleachers.

He tells my parents I have talent and asks their permission to coach me. When my parents agree, I feel special, like the star my dad says I can be.

A few years later, we move out of my grandpa's house to our new home. There, my father plants some grass in our yard so I can have my own stadium!

It rains one night and the new grass is wet, but I can wait no longer. I invite friends from my school and neighborhood to Neymar's Stadium. Everyone's happy to play on grass instead of the muddy street. But when they leave, I look at the trampled grass. I know I will be in trouble.

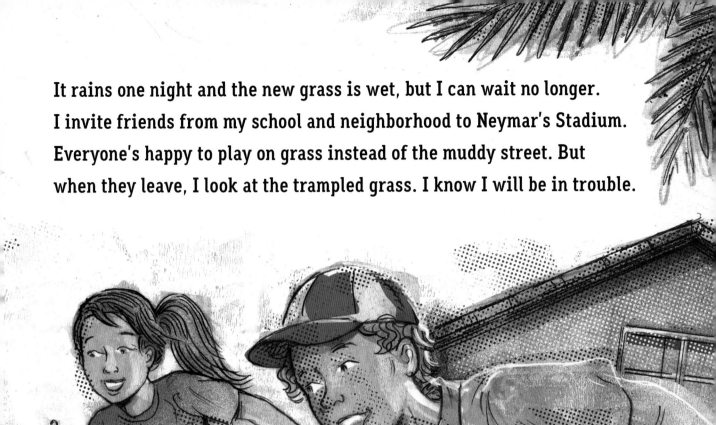

I am afraid to face my father. For days, I go to bed early, before he arrives home from work. But soon I miss playing soccer with my dad, so I stay up to see him.

"Juninho, I built this field for us so we could practice together," my father says. "You have ruined it with carelessness. A star must show self-control."

I apologize and I promise to wait until the grass grows before we play on it again.

My training finally pays off! The local soccer team, Santos FC, wants me.
They even create a new division of the youth league just so I can play.
Coach Lima says I'll be a star, but I will never forget the streets where
I learned the rhythms of soccer.

Sometimes my mom drives me to trainings, and sometimes Betinho does. But I like it best when my father doesn't work late, and my parents can take me together.

At Santos FC, I get paid a bit. I run and train where my idols Pelé and Robinho once played. I'm a happy player in a happy home, a volcano erupting with joy.

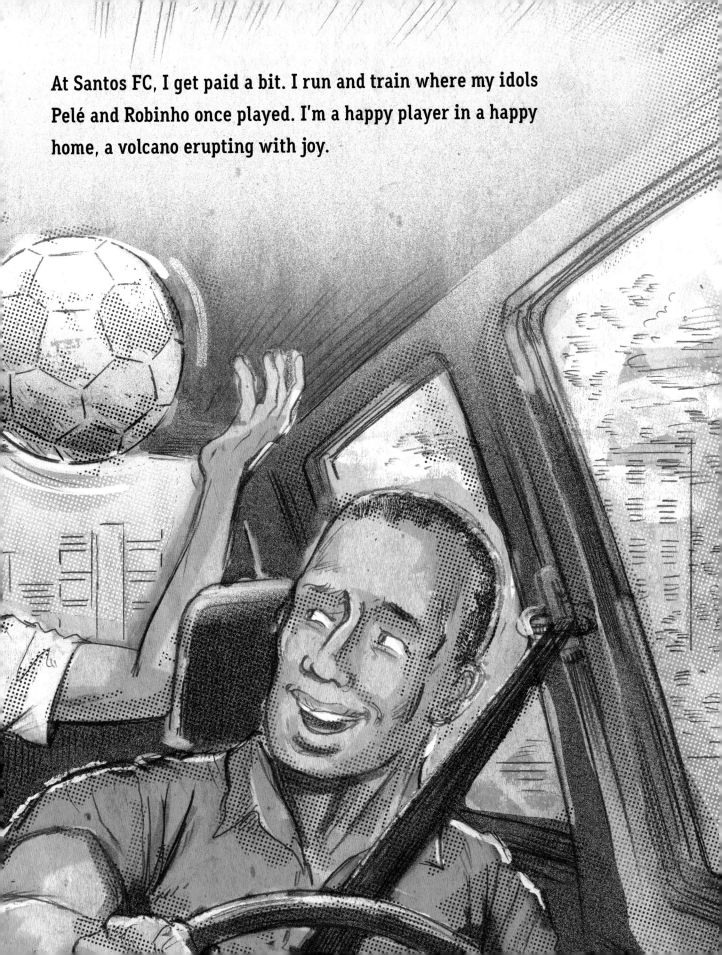

Two years after I start at Santos, Real Madrid's academy invites me to play in Spain!

"Juninho, you are my dream come true!" my father announces with pride.

Everyone knows Real Madrid means money, fame, and stardom. My father and I fly to Europe. I have never been on a plane before.

Spain is very far from Brazil. I miss my mom and my sister.

My dad knows me well. He sees I'm homesick, and he tells me that we don't have to stay in Spain.

So we pack our bags for home. I cannot wait to eat my mom's *farofa* and to play with my friends in the street.

My family, friends, and many coaches cannot believe we returned. Some disagree with my father for bringing me back to Brazil.

"Juninho is happier playing with his friends and growing up among family," my father tells them, and I listen with joy.

I play for Santos FC once again, and my game improves every day. Right after I turn seventeen, Zito knocks on our door. He is a legendary player and a manager at Santos. He invites me to play for Santos's major league, and I accept. My father thinks Zito should treat us to lunch to celebrate the occasion. But Zito would rather stay and eat my mom's cooking. So would I!

"Leftover *empadas* from
Neymar's birthday!"
my mother announces.

I adore playing ball and can run fast, but my family is my real joy.

They root for me when I help my team win the Copa Libertadores, a cup Santos had won only when Pelé played on the team. Pelé watches me lead Santos to victory. We celebrate together because we have both made history. There is no stopping me now.

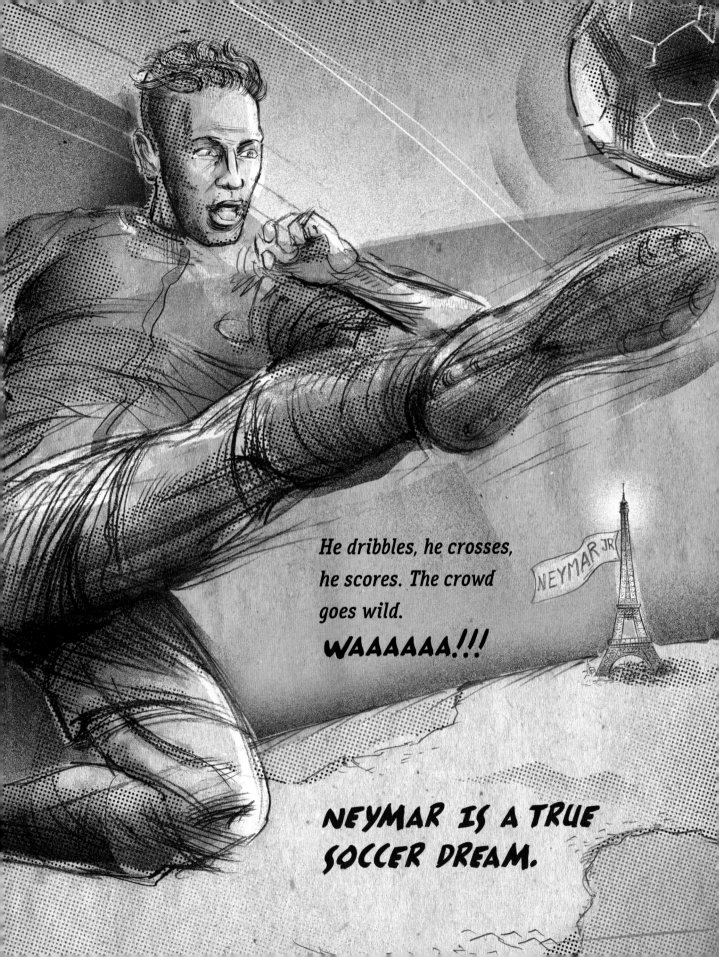

To Nathaniel, who inspired me —M.J.
To Theo —P.H.

AUTHOR'S NOTE

Soccer is more than a game I love. To me, it means being with my father. I'll never forget the first time my father took me to the Amjadieh Stadium in Tehran and the two of us watched an important match between the national teams of Iran and South Korea. As Neymar was encouraged by his father to become a soccer star, I was encouraged by my father to become a soccer fan.

It's only appropriate that one of my favorite soccer stars is Neymar, a Brazilian player, because my father also loved a Brazilian soccer player, a man called Pelé. Pelé was a star before Neymar was even born, but both men are adored in Brazil and both played for Santos FC. While I was doing research in order to write this book, I felt an even greater connection to Neymar upon finding out that he and I had both played pretend soccer matches when we were little. Neymar played with his sister and cousins, while I played with my uncle. In our games, we each took the role of the announcer, the referee, and the star. Neymar grew up to be a real soccer star, and I grew up to be an author.

This book is a creative interpretation of Neymar's life as the illustrator, Paul Hoppe, and I envision it. There is much more to Neymar and his story, of course, and although the events chronicled in this book actually happened, the dialogue is not composed of direct quotes. Rather, it is inspired by the accounts I read of Neymar's life. These are the words I imagine him saying.

GLOSSARY

Portuguese is the main language spoken in Brazil, and this book uses some Portuguese words. Here are their definitions in English:

empada: This Brazilian dish is similar to a potpie, and can be made with either savory or sweet filling.

farofa: This popular side dish is made of cassava flour and fat, like butter or bacon. Recipes are enhanced by adding eggs, chopped onions, peppers, and more. It is always served with *feijoada*.

feijoada: This bean stew with beef and pork is so popular in Brazil that it's considered the country's national dish.

Mamãe: Mom

Juninho: Junior

Seleção: This is the name of Brazil's national soccer team. Translated literally, it means "selection."

Farrar Straus Giroux Books for Young Readers
An imprint of Macmillan Publishing Group, LLC
175 Fifth Avenue, New York, NY 10010

Text copyright © 2018 by Mina Javaherbin
Pictures copyright © 2018 by Paul Hoppe
All rights reserved
Color separations by Embassy Graphics
Printed in China by Toppan Leefung Printing Ltd., Dongguan City, Guangdong Province
Designed by Monique Sterling
First edition, 2018

1   3   5   7   9   10   8   6   4   2

mackids.com

Library of Congress Control Number: 2017955301

ISBN: 978-0-374-31066-0

Our books may be purchased in bulk for promotional, educational, or business use. Please contact your local bookseller or the Macmillan Corporate and Premium Sales Department at (800) 221-7945 ext. 5442 or by e-mail at MacmillanSpecialMarkets@macmillan.com.

J-B
NEYMAR
461-9402